WHERE'S THE
TOILET ROLL?

ORCHARD

ORCHARD BOOKS

First published in Great Britain in 2020

by The Watts Publishing Group

1 3 5 7 9 10 8 6 4 2

© 2020 The Watts Publishing Group Limited

Illustrations by Dynamo Limited

Additional images © Shutterstock

A CIP catalogue record for this book is available from the British Library

ISBN 978 1 40836 397 3

Printed and bound in Italy

FSC
www.fsc.org
MIX
Paper from
responsible sources
FSC® C104740

Orchard Books
An imprint of Hachette Children's Group
Part of The Watts Publishing Group Limited
Carmelite House
50 Victoria Embankment
London EC4Y 0DZ

An Hachette UK Company
www.hachette.co.uk

WHERE'S THE TOILET ROLL?

MEET THE FRIENDS

Timmy Toilet Roll has challenged his trusty gang of poo friends to an epic game of hide and seek. Meet the contestants below, then turn the page to start the game.

TIMMY

This sensible guy likes to follow rules and can get wound up when his friends don't stick to them.

BOBBI

A true hide and seek champion. Bobbi's incredible sense of smell helps her sniff out a hiding poo from miles away.

DUCKIE

Hard to find because he's always off looking for his next adventure – preferably one where he can make a splash!

SUPERPOO

This fabulous poo's super powers give him the edge over his teammates. No game is too tricky for this hide and seek hero.

QUEENIE

Regal and calm, Queenie is a hide and seek star. She always looks for the most comfortable hiding place.

ELVIS

A mover and shaker, Elvis isn't the best at hide and seek, but he loves to try.

LUCY LOO BRUSH

Lucy is often clearing up after her poo friends. See if you can spot her in one of the scenes, too!

DUCKING AND DIVING

Duckie got his wish for a watery adventure and he couldn't be happier. Who wants a ride on his rubber ring?

PRINCESS AND THE POO

The poos are visiting the enchanted kingdom. Queenie would love to swap her sewer for a fairytale castle. Can you find her and her friends?

PREHISTORIC POOS

The poos have found themselves in a dinosaur stampede. Spot them, quick, before the dinosaurs smell them!

Odd one out!

Which dinosaur looks different from the rest?

DON'T PET THE POOS

Bobbi has taken her friends to the petting zoo. It can be a bit pongy, but they love all the cute critters. Timmy is trying to stay out of the mud.

POOS, AHOY

Watching the sailors heading out to sea, Elvis fancies life on the ocean waves. Find him and the others in the busy port. All aboard!

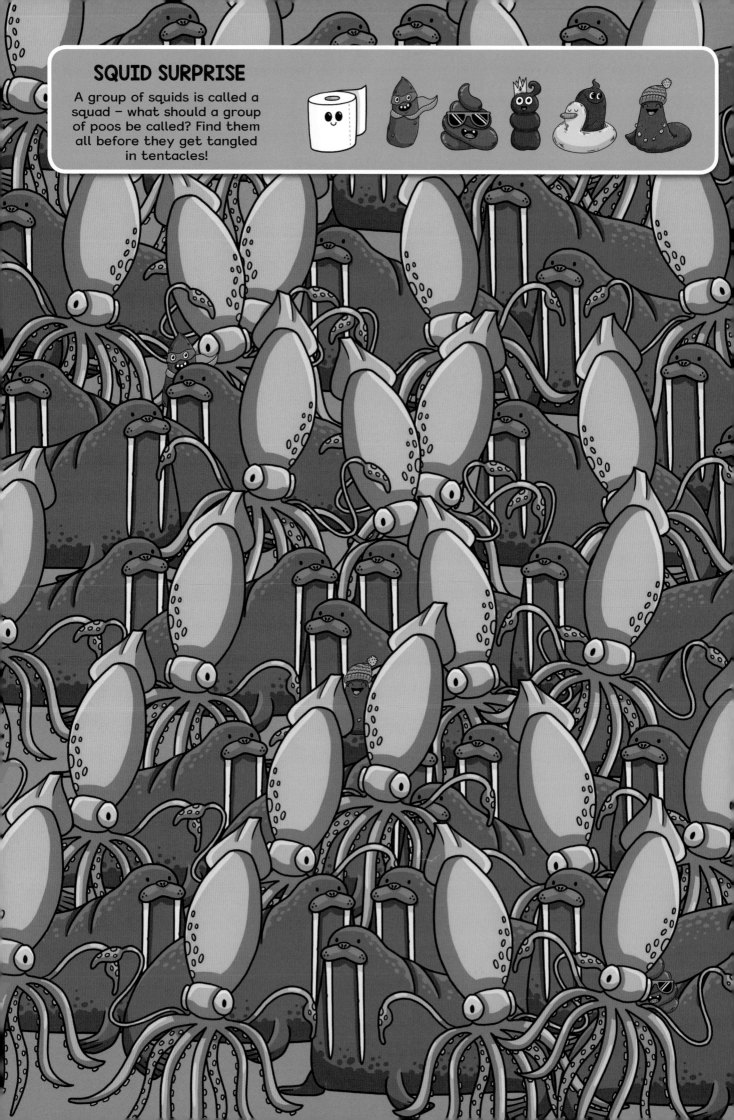

SQUID SURPRISE

A group of squids is called a squad – what should a group of poos be called? Find them all before they get tangled in tentacles!

SUPERMARKET SCAMPER

It's mayhem in the supermarket as everyone rushes to find all the items on their shopping list. Spot Timmy and his friends hiding in the aisles.

ROCK AND ROLL

Elvis is putting on a festival for all his friends. Bobbi's enjoying a boogie while Timmy's soaking up the atmosphere.

UNICORN MUDDLE

Which is rarer – a group of unicorns or a group of poos? Now you have both! Spot the poos hiding among the hooves.

Odd one out!

One of the unicorns doesn't look quite right. Can you spot it?

TOILET TOYS

Timmy and the crew are doing a spot of shopping. Queenie would like a set of walkie talkies so she can give orders without leaving her throne.

POOS GO WEEEEEE

Superpoo slips and slides around the waterpark, looking out for friends in danger. Bobbi looks like she could do with a hand – Superpoo to the rescue!

WHALE OF A TIME

Wow, these whales are enormous! Careful not to get squished, gang! Spot all the poos among the blubber.

Odd one out!

Spot the
odd whale out!

RUBBER RING RAPIDS

Duckie swerves and glides along the choppy water – he's a real daredevil. Timmy, on the other hand, is trying to stay dry! Can you find all the poos having fun?

POOS ON A PLANE

After an exhausting game of hide and seek, Timmy and the poos are heading off on holiday. But they can't resist one last go. Can you spot them hiding at the airport?

Answers

Now try and find these extra items in every scene!

DUCKING AND DIVING

Two red coral ☐

Six grey angler fish ☐

Seven shells ☐

Eight green eels ☐

Six green algae ☐

Eleven pink fish with green stripes ☐

A blue anemone ☐

Two swordfish ☐

An orange sea monster ☐

Four squid ☐

PRINCESS AND THE POO

Five owls ☐

Eight dragonflies ☐

Sixteen butterflies ☐

Two dragons ☐

Fifteen knights ☐

Two robins ☐

Twenty one toadstools ☐

Seventeen gold crowns ☐

Eight mice wearing neckerchiefs ☐

Two spiders ☐

PREHISTORIC POOS

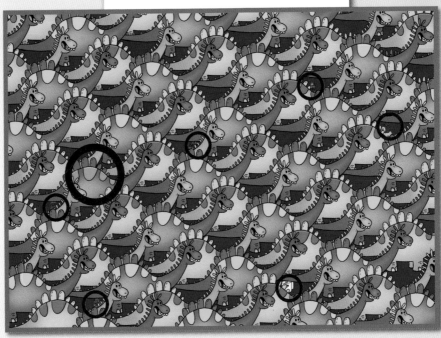

DON'T PET THE POOS

Six cabbages ☐

Fourteen carrots ☐

Five peacocks ☐

Nine turtles ☐

A black cat ☐

Three guinea pigs ☐

Twenty-one grey birds ☐

Two white rabbits ☐

Nine chirping chicks ☐

Four cows ☐

POOS, AHOY

- Nine circular windows ☐
- Two starfish ☐
- Three pairs of binoculars ☐
- Six dolphins ☐
- Three seagulls sitting on buoys ☐
- Two divers ☐
- Six life rings ☐
- Five periscopes ☐
- Four dogs ☐
- A bird wearing a captain's hat ☐

SQUID SURPRISE

SUPERMARKET SCAMPER

Two dinosaurs pushing trolleys	☐
Four American footballs	☐
Five bananas	☐
Three till points	☐
A woman wearing a blue headband	☐
Thirteen loaves of bread	☐
Three rotisserie chickens	☐
A butternut squash	☐
Two pineapples	☐
A hockey stick	☐

ROCK AND ROLL

A man blowing bubbles	☐
Four dinosaur balloons	☐
Four bananas	☐
A basketball	☐
Four birds	☐
Three deck chairs	☐
Three pink balloons	☐
Ten hay bales	☐
Six juggling balls	☐
Two face-painted tigers	☐

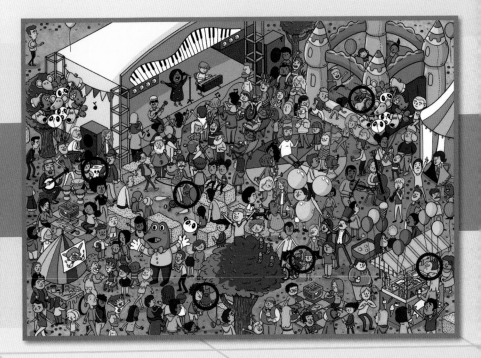

UNICORN MUDDLE

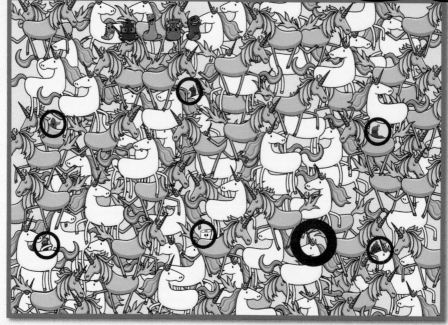

TOILET TOYS

Seven mermaids ☐

Seven dark blue ponies ☐

Six shuttlecocks ☐

Ten footballs ☐

Six trumpets ☐

Seven skittles ☐

Nine roller skates ☐

Six pots of red paint ☐

Six purple penguins ☐

Two stuffed dog toys ☐

POOS GO WEEEEEE

Six parasols ☐

A swimming unicorn ☐

Three bottles of sun cream ☐

Six snorkelling masks ☐

Three red flags ☐

A blue ice lolly inflatable ☐

Four swimming caps ☐

Four starfish ☐

A crocodile inflatable ☐

A rubber dingy ☐

WHALE OF A TIME

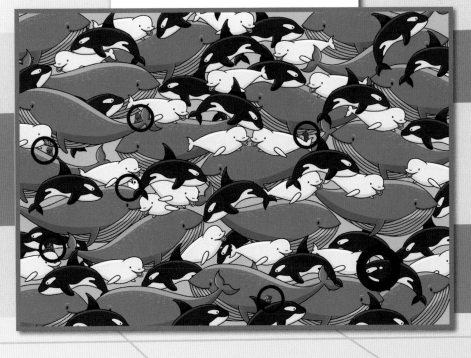

RUBBER RING RAPIDS

Three seagulls ☐

Three dolphins ☐

Two people in the water ☐

One pair of binoculars ☐

Five yellow boats ☐

Sixteen trees ☐

A man eating a picnic ☐

Two white balls ☐

Two cats ☐

A purple rucksack ☐

POOS ON A PLANE

A muffin ☐

Six coffee cups ☐

A set of footprints ☐

Six prams ☐

Two people reading newspapers ☐

A person wearing a red and blue top ☐

A person wearing a straw hat ☐

Twelve people with moustaches ☐

A picture of a sailing boat ☐

Two people holding passports ☐